D0104376

Black Sabbatical

Black Sabbatical

poems by Brett Eugene Ralph

Sarabande Books
LOUISVILLE, KENTUCKY

Managing Editor
Sarabande Books, Inc.
2234 Dundee Road, Suite 200
Louisville, KY 40205

Library of Congress Cataloging-in-Publication Data

Ralph, Brett Eugene.
    Black sabbatical : poems / by Brett Eugene Ralph. — 1st ed.
        p.   cm. — (The Linda Bruckheimer series in Kentucky literature)
    ISBN 978-1-932511-73-4 (pbk. : acid-free paper)
    I. Title.
    PS3618.A456B56 2009
    811'.6—dc22   2008040834

Cover art: "Crossing the Ohio" by Danny Lyon. Provided courtesy of Edwynn Houk Gallery and the artist.

Manufactured in Canada
This book is printed on acid-free paper.

Sarabande Books is a nonprofit literary organization.

The Kentucky Arts Council, a state agency in the Commerce Cabinet, provides operational support funding for Sarabande Books with state tax dollars and federal funding from the National Endowment for the Arts, which believes that a great nation deserves great art.

for my mother and father
and to all my teachers

CONTENTS

He, restless,
Wingless,
Hungry for more than ravage, food or flight.

—Charles Olson

FIRM AGAINST THE PATTERN

When I saw Charity dancing
alone in the farmhouse kitchen—
eyes closed, lips parted, held aloft
in one hand half a mango,
a gigantic butcher knife
clutched in the other—I froze
at the screen door as I always do
when I come upon someone praying.

All night I had been hitting
on the daughter of a tiny woman
orphaned by Hiroshima.
Grandparents had been lost, and the mother
would soon be dead though no one knew
if it was the blast or the facility
she retired next to in Utah.

This was the kind of bitter irony
that made you want to burn the flag—
even if it was against the law, even
on the Fourth of July on property owned
by a Republican state senator.
Which is precisely what would happen
later, after we'd drunk the wine.

I

Hey, he said in one of those voices
unique to fraternity members
high on nitrous oxide, *anybody want a drink
of hundred-year-old Romanian wine?*
Before we could answer, he had produced
from one of the pockets on his wheelchair
wine he meted out, so help me God,
from a Mrs. Butterworth's bottle.

By the time that bottle made its way
around the bonfire, I was drunk
on kimonos wed to atom bombs
and motherless children left to cultivate
an excruciating beauty,
drunk on crippled tipplers
scarcely larger than dolls.

Like the wine my father fashioned
out of blackberries, out of plums,
it was sweet and very strong
and it wouldn't have taken much to turn
Mrs. Butterworth upside down
until her skirts fell and I'd forgotten
that the cloud above Nagasaki rhymes
with the flag we raised on the moon.

As I watched Charity dance, I rested
my brow against the rusty screen
and that knife and mango might have been
a bottle and a beating heart,

a bomb and a burned up baby doll,
a flag and whatever comes to mind
when you read the word *forgiveness.*

Closing my eyes, I extended my tongue
and pressed it firm against the pattern:
I tasted yesterday's rain,
the carcasses of moths,
broken glances, tears,
the smoke of not-so-distant fires—
all those desperate gestures
we collect and call the seasons.

ONLY CHILD

There's so much I could tell you,
fingernail of my fingernail,
bloodshot pupil of my bloodshot eyes.

A house built itself up gradually
over dead dogs with tree-limb altars,
over hibernating yellow jackets,
over delicate tensions we
burn off like a tick at the temple. Oh,

where were you when the old man crept naked
through the house with his .38,
swearing there was a faucet on somewhere—
we'd been robbed and the sorry son of a bitch
had the gall to drink a glass of our water.
This dragged on into the winter.

The cold brought out the worst
in anybody.
A child got beaten unconscious
in December, with a snow shovel.
A child hid himself in the bushes
with a high-powered pellet rifle
he pumped as if loading a shotgun shell—

a Buddhist might call it karma, what happened,
the snow flying all around.

But what would your expression be
for the way his ankles were tightly bound
with a piece of chopped-off hose?
As he was dragged through the dirty snow,
what would you have whispered,
face I have never seen,
sister I keep on missing?

You're the one I always wanted—
the grapevine that taught me how to fall,
the graveyard I call my garden.

SPOOKY

I had never kissed a woman
with a ring through her nose, and while
what I know of farms or rodeos
wouldn't fill a flaring nostril,
something in me conjured up
the classic image of a bull.
With its onyx hooves, I saw the beast
paw the dust methodically,
little mushroom clouds to match the blue
blasts that billowed, that obscured its eyes.

I asked her if it was real,
had she invented it on the spot,
but *Spooky* seemed to suit her,
all grown up and having declared
a war against her wholesomeness—
an apple with an ice pick in it.

Let's fight! she said when she first took me
back to her room, a riot
of tattered magazines and rusted drums.
Like a child might hug a tree,
she tackled me around my waist,
and if she was small, she was equally strong—
the proof a black eye from a head butt

as I tried to pin her elbows
to the bed on which we'd fallen.

At Swiss Hall, as we sat huddled
in a booth back near the bar,
she slapped me hard and with a smile
said, *I bet that surprised you!*

I had to read her lips above the roar
of a terrible metal band
and the handprint I felt spreading
its red cape across my face.

I awoke on sticky carpet, wedged between
a wall and the capsized mattress.
Spooky splashed in the tub, and I tried
to fix it before she finished,
but the bed collapsed into the table,
scattered its bonbons and spiral notebooks,
its cracked china and crumpled underthings.

Whether we broke her bed
or only knocked it off its pedestal
that night, there's no telling.
But something led me to believe
it happened before I got there. Led me to believe
it had been broken all along.

THE STUDENT

has a question
you don't know the answer to.
You scan the immaculate shelves—there
is comfort between those covers.

You linger on a slender volume
given years ago,
yet you can recite each letter
penned inside.

She is saying
your name now, the student,
the strap of her purse encircling
a thin, freckled wrist.
You tell her it's okay
to write about her abortion.

As she presses on, you can't help
but wonder about the father—
whether he's a student, too,
maybe one of yours. A face
appears: a young man you despise
for reasons you forget.
It's his face you picture as she's breaking
the news; his face, remote as a pistol
dropped over the side of a boat.

She knows how precious it is,
she says, and thanks you for your time.
Slowly you pass your hand
over the smooth, passive spines,
her body echoing down the corridor.

Then you retrieve a book you need
not ever read again, let alone
the inscription—burned in
like a star's trajectory, still there
when you close your eyes, you see the shape
of the mouth that mouthed it,
you can't help but hear
that voice.

       You wonder
if she is crying, too—
your student.

And what does that make you.

Artificial Starling

The bleachers are abandoned
yet the stadium fills—
something pumped in,
something planned.

Scientists keep inventing
new ways to be afraid. How
droppings deface our sidewalks
and befoul the immaculate grass,
dribbled from Pollocked awnings that embellish the dark
cottages wherein we eke out sleep.

How we cannot help but carry it
indoors, encrusted on boot-soles, blown
like ash into our eyes.

When I first heard it,
I was already running.

Amplified across the campus,
infecting subdivisions,

a robot cacophony
blunt and ubiquitous as wind.

More taste than sound, it lingers:
a train-flattened penny lolled on the tongue,
copper's menstrual tang.

———————

As I circle the field, a bird is perched
atop a towering speaker.

Maybe he hears the machine
and the machine alone,
a featherless messenger,
seducing like a gruesome movie, a self-
destructive fling.

Or maybe, a-thrum in his heart,
he understands precisely
what he's hearing, and is
drawn by familiar tongues—

even those distorted
by misfortune, feeding back.
Even if it isn't real.

HOUSE OF SELECTED FLAMES

The darkness peals
as each star is inserted. Truly
stars are harmless—I mean
they only hurt themselves. Did I
mention how hot it is?

Wind dips in like a hand, places
water on the nightstand
and then runs
the length of my right leg. I follow
my thoughts a certain distance.

If you're awake
and thinking what I am thinking,
you are dead wrong—

I will not disintegrate
amidst the siren's multiple choice:
the flames doused, a life saved, possibly
locked away forever. Or, d)

all of the above. Fear is
such a dirty dress to wear;
wet across the abdomen
like a faded label that might have read
Fragile, way back when.

REINDEER GAMES

The guy with the glass eye drives.
The only one old enough,
it will be him who's blamed if things go bad,
him they'll send to jail.
They stick to back roads,
eyes peeled for pigs.

If you come after midnight, the story goes,
to the graveyard at Hot Rod Haven,
her right hand's ice to the touch, and the other
will singe your fingers.
What time is it?
Chicken Man wants to know.

Holding his wrist up to the moon,
Tucker says, *I've got good news, boys—*
it just so happens it's after midnight. It was
always after midnight.

Junior's laughing, his body hung
from the shotgun side, obliterating
mailboxes with a bat.

Tucker wants to see this and turns,
taking his eye off the road. *The two sides*
of his face aren't the same, Junior thinks.
One knows what is happening, and one
never will. Tucker looks back
to the highway just in time
not to sideswipe a station wagon.
There's laughter all around.

As they wait at the White Castle Drive-Thru,
Ricky and Chicken Man decide to catch
a ride with a couple of girls. Junior can't
go home. He tries to talk
Tucker into riding out to the radio tower.
Pulls a pen from his jacket pocket,
disassembles it. *I've been saving this*
all night for you . . . He nudges
the lighter with his knee.

———

There's no other way
to tell it: Tucker fell.

The worst part, by far, was having to climb
all the way back down.
Junior had a lot to think about,
one rung at a time—

some things made him sorry; others
made him sick.
He wondered if falling wasn't half as scary
for Tucker as anyone else.
Then he started laughing,
so hard he had to stop and hook
both elbows around the ladder.

———————

From the dewy grass, he watched the tower
jut into the dawn. He shut
his eyes and blew out his breath.

Before the darkness behind his lids
could erase the blinking beacon,
he remembered what Tucker'd told him:

He was playing chicken with his cousin
and he lost a dart in the sun.

———————

Oh man, he whispered. *Oh shit,*
Oh God—Tucker
resembled a car wreck.

Not the victim but the wreck itself.
Something had happened
to his lower half, but his arms were still intact,
thrown wildly as if he'd died cheering,
spelling out a letter. He lay
face down, thank God.
Fumbling blindly, Junior fished
the keys from Tucker's pocket.
Birds seemed to be everywhere. He wondered
how long he'd been hearing them.

Careful not to get caught on the barbwire fence,
Junior landed funny, hurt his foot.
Then he kicked at the gravel, grimacing.

He couldn't make up his mind to listen
to the radio or not. Off
and on. Then off again. Never hearing
more than half a song, a horrible
blast of static. His ankle
throbbed like a bad idea.

No one had bothered teaching Junior
how to drive a stick—
every time he tried to stop, the damned thing
just kept dying. It took forever
getting hold of somebody.

COUNTRY SONG

Rain like nails yanked out with a pair of pliers,
this sure is a lonely pasture
I pulled up next to, emptying

bottle after sweaty bottle
into myself until I get to feeling
pissed, and somewhat monastic.

And I can see her serpentine amble,
I can still hear her ticking off
the tiles with Antarctic clarity.

Those burros are just the same
and more of it, their eyes
acquiescence personified,

dead planets on which no banjo
has ever broke a string,
no waltz ever choked off

in mid-sob, no blasted mind to wonder
what the fuck they're staring at, or whether
they have ever laid eyes on anything sadder.

IN OPEN G

for Don & Phil Everly

There is a hole in my lap
the sound comes out of,
but there is no sound now.

So I turn it upside down and shake—
hear the pick's hollow rattle,
hope for it to fall.

I can't say if men still arm themselves
with picks as they embark on their dark
odyssey into the earth,

but Egypt Mines had an operation
once, when I first moved here,
butted up against my land.

On warm nights, windows open,
there was a constant, distant rumble;
transparent voices that may or may not have

bled into this world;
huge, lunar contraptions emitting
the '*mon back* beep of a garbage truck,

which by light of day resembled nothing
so much as dinosaur remains. It's less
than half an hour from my house

to the place where Isaac Everly
rose from a pit, rubbed grit from his eyes and vowed
no son of his would break his neck

sucking blood from a stone
or sing a lifelong lonesome song
underneath a mountain in blackface.

Ike would drop his pick and pluck his sons
from fields of green infinity,
the place they had ever prayed

and laid down weary heads, tried not to hear
coal trains as they hauled away
the planet's very pulse, a life

Ike's boys would never have to learn
though they'd spend the rest of their days on earth
grown filthy rich from singing

songs of longing to return.

THE DEPARTURE

The first time I brought her up,
they sat me down
in a chair from somebody's kitchen.

The boy swung
on a grape vine up above.

The man kept handing me
feathers, one at a time—I knew
what to do with them.

Later I found a photograph
taped to the bottom of the chair,
yellow a long time and nothing
to look at. Guess who
it was of?

Don't worry, the man said.
You don't know her.

I said I think I do.

The boy giggled and clapped
his tiny hands.
The man let out one of those never-ending
sighs across the centuries.

Then he stared me dead
in the face and said: *Now
why did you have to go and tell me that?*
At long last I understood
she wasn't coming back.

The man turned
into an owl and flew away.
Limb by limb, tree by tree,
the boy began to climb.

He went deep into what would have been
the forest canopy,
had it not been November—
all the leaves taken,
every nest exposed.

EMACIATED BUDDHA

Scarcely do we see him
lost in all his wandering,
dollop of cold rice in a dirty palm,
whatever slumber he can muster
hard won from snakes and rocks and seething rain,
the febrile congress of frogs, the unseen
unrest of insect worlds, the wind-
begotten complaints of the hunted, the haunted
creatures perishing in the dark.

Like Christ in Grünewald's triptych,
he looks like a man who's truly spent
a lifetime nailed to a shadeless tree:
skinny arms like tired entreaties,
face like a cave, each protruded rib
a distinct refusal, once and future
beauty of the body discarded
like a murky early draft.

FLOWERING JUDAS

Every time I open my eyes
The phantoms all expire
They could be klansmen, they could be little girls
Wearing wedding dresses

Two shadows
Mine and the cat's
Stalk the summer grasses

For turtles, dew-softened
Concert tickets, news
Of Thomas Merton

Two nights they were digging
Up against my neighbor's fence
In the morning the shovels
Were put away

They covered the hole with an old
Canvas lawn chair
Weighed down at the corners with cinder blocks

Weeds grown up so high now we'll never know
But there—long before the chair—
Merle said they was some flowers

Back on the porch
A breeze lolls
Yard to yard

Pine whisper
Thin branches only

A mourning dove emerges

Far off
The way a train sounds
The way a dog barks at night
At nobody
The way phones ring over & over when you
Almost want to answer

When it's not your phone
But you can hear it

TREE LIMBS LETTING GO OF SNOW

I fear my wife's best friend is mad.
She won't stop saying she can't believe
how wonderful her life is. She faces
my wife across our kitchen table.

The insistence in all she says
unsettles—cold words all aglare
inside, jangled signs
along a wide, wet street.

This woman spent
twenty hours on a bus so she could crawl
into our laps like a frozen animal
found in the snow, still breathing.

When my wife is talking, her friend is static—
rigid as if she were strapped to her seat.
When my wife is talking, momentarily
I can force her friend from my mind and look

past her, to the clearing behind our house.
The high trees are heavy
with all they can hold of last night's snow.
I am so thankful my wife is not crazy,

so grateful to be drifting,
so glad that I'm not dead,
kicked in the neck by a thoroughbred
like this woman's husband was.

The wind sweeps snow
from an upper branch, and it holds
a form like a ghost across the clearing.
As far as I am able, I follow it

until it passes into the distant pines.

GREAT HORNED VISITATION

A deep, clicking hiccup
some place outside my bedroom.

I lay the book aside and gently
pull a window down:

nothing. Then I hear it,
louder than before, like it is

clinging to my curtains.
For a long time, I close my eyes

and listen for its call,
for others calling back in kind

across equivocal distance.
But I need to *see* the thing,

so I snatch the flash light by my bed,
kick the dogs inside as I

ease the screen door shut.
Inched to porch's edge—a sound

so deep it makes me shiver
as I did when I had seen a hawk,

beneath a neighbor's tree, slowly
disembowel a dove.

Underneath the evergreen
right outside my room, I glimpse

barred wings wider than wings should be,
no more noise than a sigh

from the precipice of sleep.
Late once, alone, another night,

from a roadside ditch, a ghostly blur
arose and crossed my hood to glance

without a sound against the windshield.
In the weeds it wasn't hard to find,

and when I held it in my hands,
unmarred and mollified, it seemed

almost impossibly small. I knew
what to call it, but what are we

that such magnificent creatures have to die
before they'll let us touch them.

TELL CITY

Somebody stripped
the bark from the trees. It's worse
than being burned. For reasons
we needn't go into
I'm assuming it was a man.

Just think of everything he had
to abandon to the periphery: friends
he lost the number of,
the desk he left swimming
in manuscripts,
the appropriated car
he parked in a ditch and left,
running.

In tow, a translucent
garbage bag. A lazy man
might call it silver, might say
it's gray, the look on his face
as he forces
his nails into the elm.

He has no name for this,
unless there's a word for what you see
profiled in a horse's eye,

locked in a stall, the stable ablaze—you know,
the one the cowboy can't get to.

I want to ask how he decided
who to give up on first:
Does one discover
some kind of order?—

or just dart in
like a man in a barn on fire.

THIS POEM HAS A HOLE IN THE MIDDLE

There are no metaphors
for what was done to her.
The seven boys who pushed her off
her bike, her school books splayed
like poisoned pigeons on the pavement—

those boys are not symbolic.
They are real,
and this poem has a hole in the middle,
a hollow tree stuffed with *Hustlers*, deep
in the woods beyond the subdivision;

a sofa sagging
in the family room, bathed
in late-night TV's purple light—
when it went black
before your parents came back

and the babysitter got bored.
Television didn't cost anything
yet, and your options could be counted on
the fingers of one hand.
And even if you didn't want to

because you didn't understand,
even if you hated it more than anything

in the world, whatever they showed,
you had to sit through
because you were just a child.

DONKEY

I used to see you out in the field
conducting insects with your ears.
Sun slowly sharpened
the stripe across your shoulders
and you swallowed sleep through your eyeholes.

Shifting weight to your forelegs
you lifted your head from the tender grass
and thrust it forward, long neck bulging
as a series of sharp, moist, muscular spasms,
lip-sprung, ruptured the air.

Underlying all that violence, there
seemed to be a kind of laughter—it wasn't
malicious, it wasn't apologetic.
I closed my eyes and leaned my arms
against the fence and listened.

Your voice did not disturb me then.
It was something that had to happen:
Heavy limbs loosed
at last from the trunk. Ice
unfreezing all at once.

I hear it different in the city,
mingled with the spit of helicopters,

the giggle of broken glass.
It's like somebody choking on a car horn
or something metal being born.

REAL NUMBERS

How long the night to the watchman,
How long the road to the weary traveler,
How long the wandering of many lives
To the fool who misses the way.

—Dhammapada

A dull thing fluttered close
and I jerked, jostling my companion,
who muttered, *Fucking watch it!*—who knelt
at the bottom stair.

I squatted, a hunter wondering
just what my buddy'd bagged
in that Bardo of deep freeze
and cinder block, of pipes
resurrected by duct tape, an ancient
latticework of webs.

In other words,
we snorted crystal meth
right off the concrete steps.
God knows the slivers,
how much grit,
which inscrutable organism
I invited in. Anything

wears off, I realize, given time—
anything cooked up in a bath tub

35

at a farm house no one owns.
But what about the glittering,
living things?

Like monks who copy a manuscript
over and over until the words are random
scratches made by a razor, we
hunkered down until we rose
into a room unrecognizable, emptied
of everyone save ourselves.

But before we'd risen,
before we'd busted our tongues
in the throes of so many sentences,
I glanced at the filthy light
where countless tiny lives had ended
and knew I would stay awake to see
the sun spill its syrup
across the convenience mart parking lot,
knew I'd taste the blade on my tongue.

Before a five dollar bill could disappear
into my face, this faint vagabond
started listing my direction,
and somehow I knew that stranger
would fix me with a stare,
holding me as ferociously
as she clung to the bars of the bike she pushed,
shoe-stringed and heaped to the point of collapse
with all manner of earthly possession.

HANDICAPPED VAN CONVERSION

I was just riding around
peering into yards,
starved for a toy,

a lawn chair.
It was dusk, nearly
dinner time.

I cut my engine, hidden
by a hunching sycamore.
The slow strobe of the television lit

a picture window, the whole front room
an intermittent blue
like faces after my accident.

I had no desire to know them—
one efficient with fork and knife, so careful
not to upset his tray; the other

down on the floor, Indian style, in her lap
a plate piled high—yet I wanted
more than life to be bathed

blue, alongside the two of them.
I wanted to sit on their couch
and eat off my knees.

I wanted news,
any kind of news.
I wanted to know what was happening

to everyone else.

MUDRA

The machine spit out my solitary
dollar bill. I smoothed it against my Levi's,
moistened my fingertips, wet the edge.
When it emerged a second time, and a third,
hanging like a tongue, I saw myself
speckled with blood and Pepsi, saw
the gashes this machine would make
as I dismantled it with my hands.

She was a brown-haired girl near the exit,
hands folded neatly in her lap.
But the look on her face when I opened my mouth—
there was something odd about it:

You don't have any change, do you?

I shifted from foot to foot,
watched as she withdrew
from her coat a little purse, a kind
you hardly ever see.
The kind my mother gave me once
to keep my marbles in.

She unsnapped it and started
to pluck out coins. One by one, she felt
along their edges, thumbed each face,

her own face empty as it fed her fingers,
tabulating, dropping change
into the valley of her skirt.

I think I've got it, yes, she said,
smiling up at me. She scooped
the coins, rolled them slowly
into the cup I'd made of my hands.

Perfect—I jingled them—*thanks a lot;*
I pressed a dollar in her palm.
You're welcome, I heard her say,
after I'd turned already, fed my buck
into the face of the machine.

I could say that her cane's gentle tapping
resembled the first few drops of rain
on the roof of an aluminum trailer,
nuggets in the pan of a prospector,
dimes in a hobo's cup; I can reckon
how much it all was worth,
and I bet I'd still feel guilty—

for had I figured it out beforehand,
I never even would've asked
and might have lost my chance to see
each coin honored like a shard
of bone on a Buddhist rosary,
her face suffused with simple attention
and, to my eyes, a kind of bliss.

THE MAN

Looks kinda familiar, could be
just about anybody. That fella
in the cafeteria, sucking
his french fries in silence; that face
in the darkened pharmacy—
the glass again three-dimensional
as you slowly back away; the mumbling
stumbler who comes at you
with a bloody broken bottle
he turns into a rose (or is it
the other way around?); any way
you look at it, just as red—
as irresistible as red
things have to be, thornless
or no, no horns
that show, shorn of any
tell-tale signs: you won't know him
when you see him. You didn't
even when you did.

ELEGY FOR LORRI

One time we got high
together in the bathroom stall
of a bar. There was trouble
keeping it lit, so when I'd had my hit
I hurried, holding it up
to where your lips were.

Black Sabbatical

Those magnolias are
immaterial—they don't give a shit
about the seasons. It's fall,
just in case you're wondering.

The lips of the windows
moisten: They are ready
to single me out. There
is one cloud, and it knows

no boundaries. It follows
like the little sister who wants you to
buy her booze. News-
papers compose themselves,

heedless to the traffic.
Among crippling ideas,
a decent excuse—
a solitary star.

I'm free to prostrate myself
on the sidewalk, an acorn
consummated by raindrops,
free to lap like a stray

at an oil-emblazoned puddle.
No one takes note of me—
a miracle! Nobody
inks my name, neatly

folding it away. I slip
into an unattended vehicle, sleep
until trees snap like wet pencils
and the last bits of advice have been given.

HEAVEN OF EXTINCTION

We are, most of us, so busy searching
for spigots marked *honey* and *milk*, for bodiless
choirs emitting unearthly scales,
for everyone who owes us money,
those unrequited adolescent crushes
totaled in gleaming pickups,
so distracted that we never stray
into sanctuaries where long gone species
of this world go on living.

Toddlers stolen by polio
and Legionnaire's Disease
scramble after lurid butterflies grown
huge on heavenly nectar.
Crack babies trample the myriad grasses
incompatible with cement,
shriek amid clouds of Chestnut Leafwings
and Nogales Metalmarks.

Near the treeline lurk Christian Scientists,
hillbillies, those who saw fit to refuse
treatment in times of plague.
They reach into pockets that never empty,
scatter seed for Heath Hen and Solitaire
and Passenger Pigeons not consigned to carry
divine communiqués.

Wherever rivers twist through paradise,
sprawled on mossy rocks are kids
who smuggled weapons into school
and every single person that suffered
from road rage, whether or not they died
out there on the highway. They are free
to lie on their bellies, chin on hand, and watch
Pupfish worry the surface,
Harelip Suckers crowd the shoals.

The ancients who, near the end of their days,
grew bitter or abusive
straddle the shells of Giant Tortoises,
who never go too fast, never forget
the short cut to the drug store.
They are borne through the forest, oblivious
to limbs alive with Djoongari
and Delta Blues Musicians,
the Lesser Mascarene Flying Fox,
the Sexy Librarians somehow
making peace with all those trees.

Because each of us goes to heaven
no matter what we've done,
the rapists and thoughtless destroyers
of little girls and boys,
those of us whose crimes remain
incomprehensible even to God,
sit on stumps and watch a Burrowing Boa
disappear into the dirt

as a Christmas Island Rat cavorts
unmolested, unaware.

They have no need of sleep, these men,
and never tire of this tableau—
they are so thankful to be thinking, finally,
of anything but themselves.

Impossible Blues

I did not cross a continent
to sing my song
in congress with caterpillars,
to watch intangible Lutherans
toss their hair and disappear
in tuberous thickets, intoxicated
with the longing that is not
longing.
          Neither did I intend
to autograph anyone's ice cream,
my body safely stowed away—
one more dirty secret
amid a cargo of long johns and donut holes.

Instead, I'll hijack
escalators, juggling griefs;
I'll swallow the graveyard,
every purple leaf. And I will eat
the deadly thing and it shall not harm me,
I'll take up serpents
stitched on golden shoulders in bold
and impossible blues.

Let junkies inhabit their sweet abyss,
let them whisper *Dee Dee's dead,*
coveting silver buckles

and immaculate cowboy boots,
their litanies bled of any temptation,
faint as thinning rain—

streaks on a stranger's window,
droplets on the screen.

POEM:

When I held her through an apocalypse,
when the years
interceded like a metal chair
thrown across a room,
you were there, nodding, definitions
spilling from your sockets.

I was down among the forsaken
pennies, the puddling ice cubes,
the nyloned foot
in search of a secret purchase . . .

You raised me up by the armpits
and kissed me, hard, on the mouth.

When I came to Butchertown, you elected
not to follow inside—stained
ceilings, ephemeral faces: hungry
ghosts disguised as bikers, punks,
coke-whores & hillbilly sociopaths.

Insects blended into the stucco;
something winged close, only to vanish
into a fissure in the air.

Sleep arrived, dimly familiar—
Hosanna of dead bolt
and twisted-down blinds, O friend, O furtive
nourishment. It was you,
your feathered susurration
through the screen as I slept. O Poem—

my mother's sad momentum;
Poem, my father's death
barreling like freight
out of the future—no words
can cushion these collisions.

But when the mind has whitewashed
its mausoleum walls
one tear at a time,
I discover, even then, a can
of spray paint in my hand.

I shake it, I train it
on burnished stone.
And while the sweating letters I leave behind
may echo another's name—

Poem, if I'm anyone's,
I'm yours.

WHIPPOORWILL

There was a time I cursed you,
closed my window
to your three shrill notes.
I wanted to fire
a pistol shot
into your sixty-minute song.

Even in sleep, when it came,
you would come to me
disguised as a telephone—a call
I'd been expecting. Afraid
to answer, afraid to know, I let you

ring through every dream.
And when my heart stopped (I'm sorry)
fluttering; when thoughts no longer
(forgive me) *flew about,*
stirred up like so much dust,

I awoke to a silence so empty
I prayed for a reprise,
even if it meant not falling
ever again to sleep
and, so deprived, I might find myself
capable of anything—
a cluster of tight-lipped

cuts above the ankle, say,
like the ones my girlfriend made.

We must select
the silences we live by,
and I won't let this be mine.
So resume your idiotic
song, and mitigate
this nothingness. Help me
find a voice among the feathers
and make of the night
a delicate thing.

DERBY EVE

No moon, nothing mirrored on the surface of the pool
save a pale form, stripped
and fixing to sink.
Later he'd slip and skin himself, toppling
to moan among wood chips. It was a song

we'd been hearing for years, our mouths
torn open as our bodies spun, haunted
and inaudible—sound
so loud it seemed impossible
it was coming from inside,
that it leapt through windows onto the patio
where the nude boy continued to writhe.

The kitchen was a lime green oasis,
its faces splayed against stove and fridge,
and I tried everything not to see
the role I assumed as I refused
the umpteenth offer of alcohol, pinched
the proffered joint and passed it on.

I rifled the cupboard, the room alive
behind me like all my reasons,
and the voices I kept hearing were bad

impressions of former selves—I'd said
all of these things a hundred times,
worn every hangdog façade.

Blame nested in my tonsils, expected to fly;
I filled my glass at the faucet,
drank it dry.

Abruptly I took my leave and entered
the deafening living room,
its population of demented mimes,
each voice swallowed up so I'm forced to read
the features of the naked man
as he kneels, still dripping, on a Persian rug.

Every gesture reads *fear*, reads
supplication, reads *Oh God, please
don't hit me, I'm drunk, I don't know
what I'm doing*—and still it shocks me
when his forehead slams
into the glass top of the coffee table.

On my way out, I avoid the mirrors
everyone keeps turning into.
Down on the street, I try to imagine
silks of myriad brilliance,
spires that pierce the sky,
gorgeous, powerful animals pounding

sun-drenched dust beneath them
as thousands upon thousands
cheer and lift their drinks.

ACKNOWLEDGMENTS

Thanks are owed to the editors of the following publications, in which some of these poems first appeared: *Elsewhere: A Journal for the Literature of Place, Harpur Palate, Marquee, McSweeney's, Moon City Review, Open 24 Hours, Pig: A Journal, Red Brick Review, The Round Table, Southern Indiana Review*, and *Willow Springs*. A number of these poems were also included in the chapbooks *Like the Bone Wants to Break Through the Skin* and *27 Years*. I am particularly grateful to the editors of Spotlight Press and White Fields Press.

I would also like to express my gratitude to the following folks for their guidance and encouragement during the writing of these poems: Ted Beck, Jonathan Bentley, David Berman, Nickole Brown, Taylor Carlisle, Michael Centore, Brian Foye, Sarah Gorham, Harold Maier, Bernd Sauermann, Jeffrey Skinner, Chris Stroffolino, James Tate, William Waltz, and Dara Wier. I am indebted especially to Michelle Tupko for her close, clear readings.

Additional thanks go to the powers that be at Hopkinsville Community College for a generous sabbatical leave that aided me in the completion of this manuscript.

Special thanks to Danny Lyon for use of the image on the cover of this book.

I am especially indebted to Linda Bruckheimer for funding the Kentucky Series in Literature.

The title "House of Selected Flames" was lifted from Lorri Jackson.

"Reindeer Games" is for Richard Peyton, who told me part of the story.

"Real Numbers": The epigraph is from Thomas Byrom's translation of *Dhammapada: The Sayings of the Buddha* (Boston: Shambala, 1993).

"Mudra" refers to a symbolic hand gesture made during Buddhist meditation.

"Impossible Blues" was commissioned by Greg Bachar.

"Elegy for Lorri": Lorri Jackson, poet (1961–1990)—*The mind is at least one room.*

"Derby Eve" is for David Berman.

THE AUTHOR

Brett Eugene Ralph spent the better part of his youth in Louisville, Kentucky, playing football and singing in punk rock bands. His work has appeared in publications such as *Conduit, Willow Springs,* and *The American Poetry Review*, and his poems have been anthologized in *The McSweeney's Book of Poets Picking Poets* and *The Stiffest of the Corpse: An Exquisite Corpse Reader.* He has taught at the University of Massachusetts, Missouri State University, and the Central Institute of Buddhist Studies in the Himalayas of northern India. Currently, he lives in Empire, Kentucky, and teaches at Hopkinsville Community College. His country rock ensemble, Brett Eugene Ralph's Kentucky Chrome Revue, can be heard in seedy dives throughout the South.

Joel McDonald